Christmas
DOT ART
Coloring Book For Kids

MW00898216

Welcome to **Little Cat Press**, where learning and playing come together in the most delightful way!

From coloring books to activity books, our high-quality books engage young readers in fun and educational activities. They encourage creativity and thinking skills while helping children identify with the world around them. Little Cat Press is dedicated to providing hours of entertainment and learning for kids of all ages.

Embark on a journey of discovery and adventure through our wonderful world of books, and help your child unlock the joy of reading and learning with Little Cat Press!

Copyright © 2023 by Little Cat Press. All rights reserved.

No part of this book may be reproduced or used in any manner without written permission from the publisher, except brief portions quoted for the purpose of review.

THIS BOOK BELONGS TO

....

....

TEST COLOR PAGE

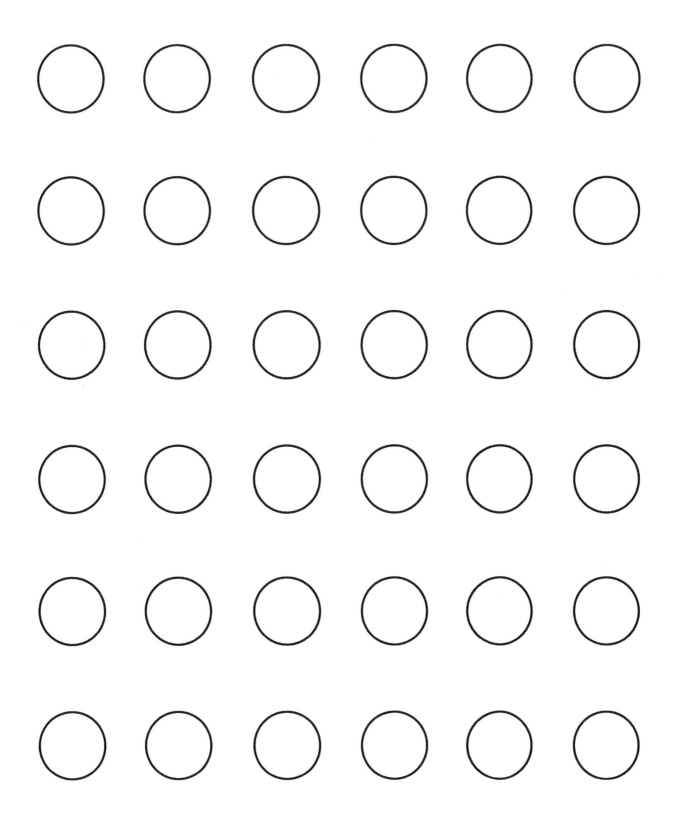

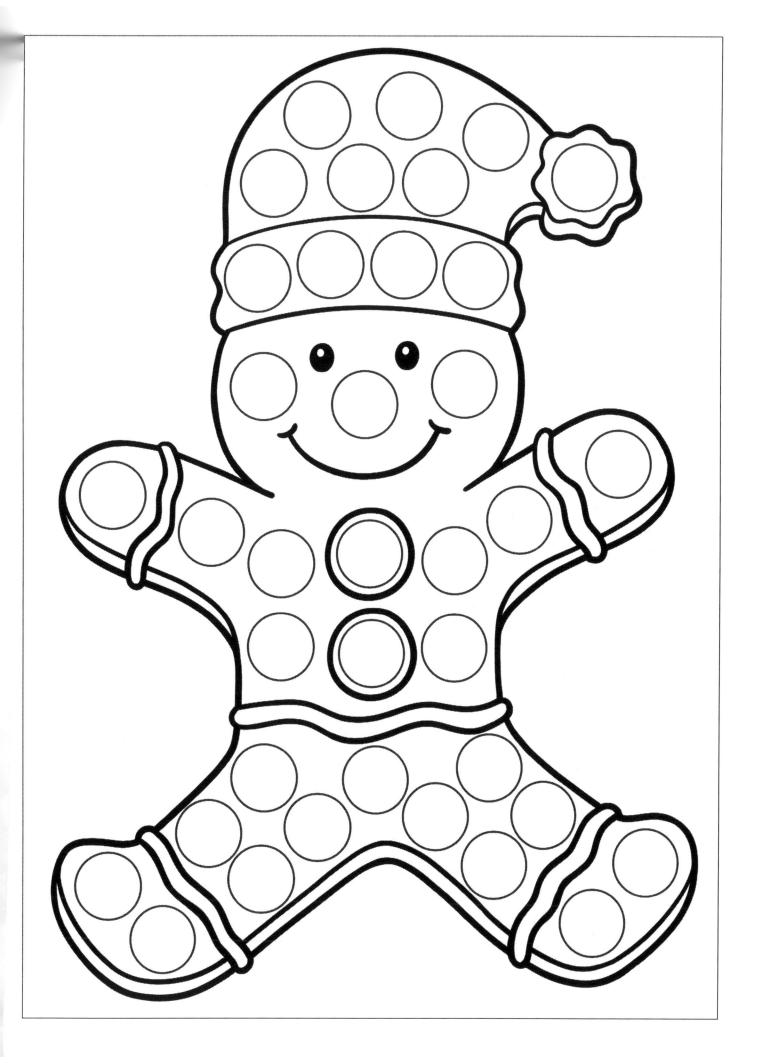

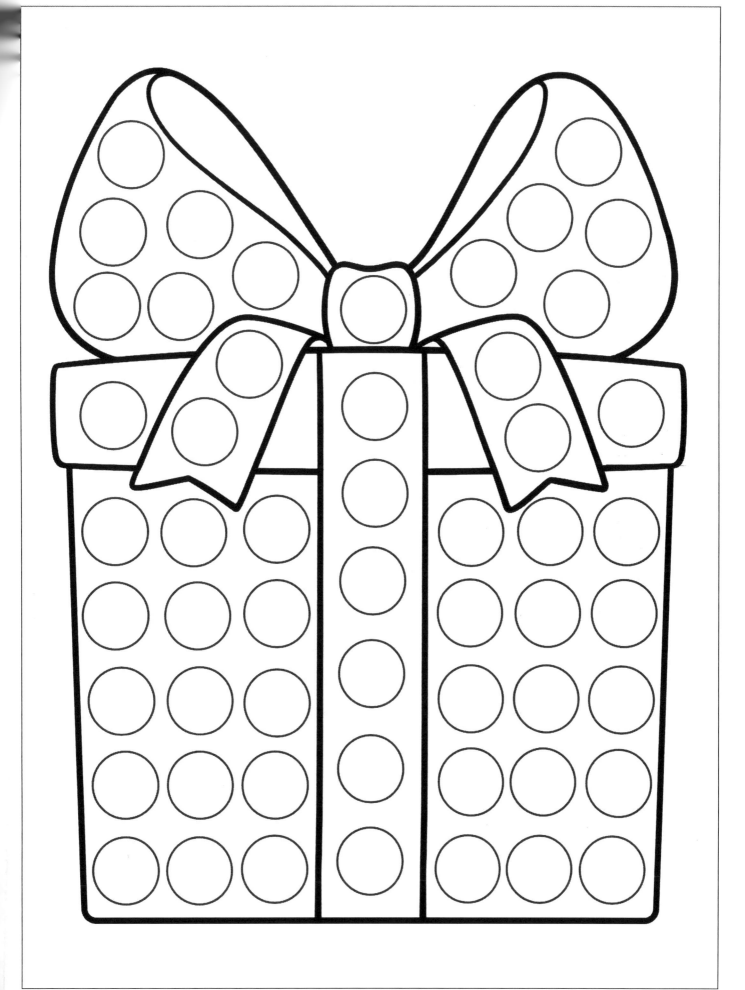

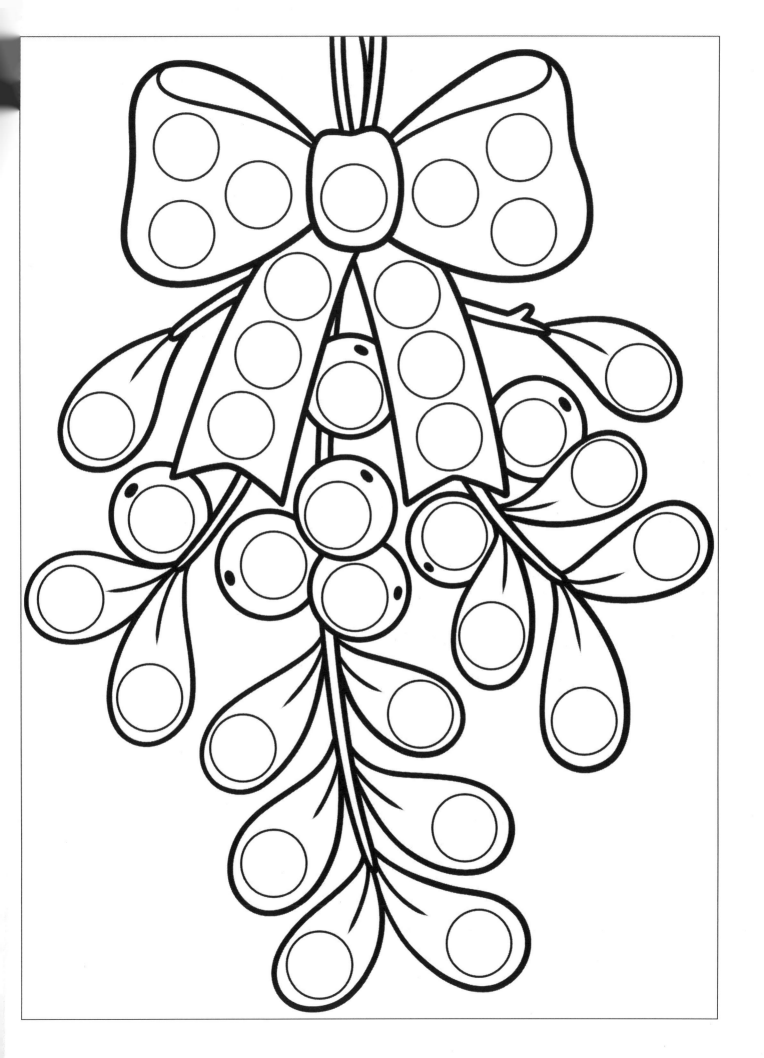

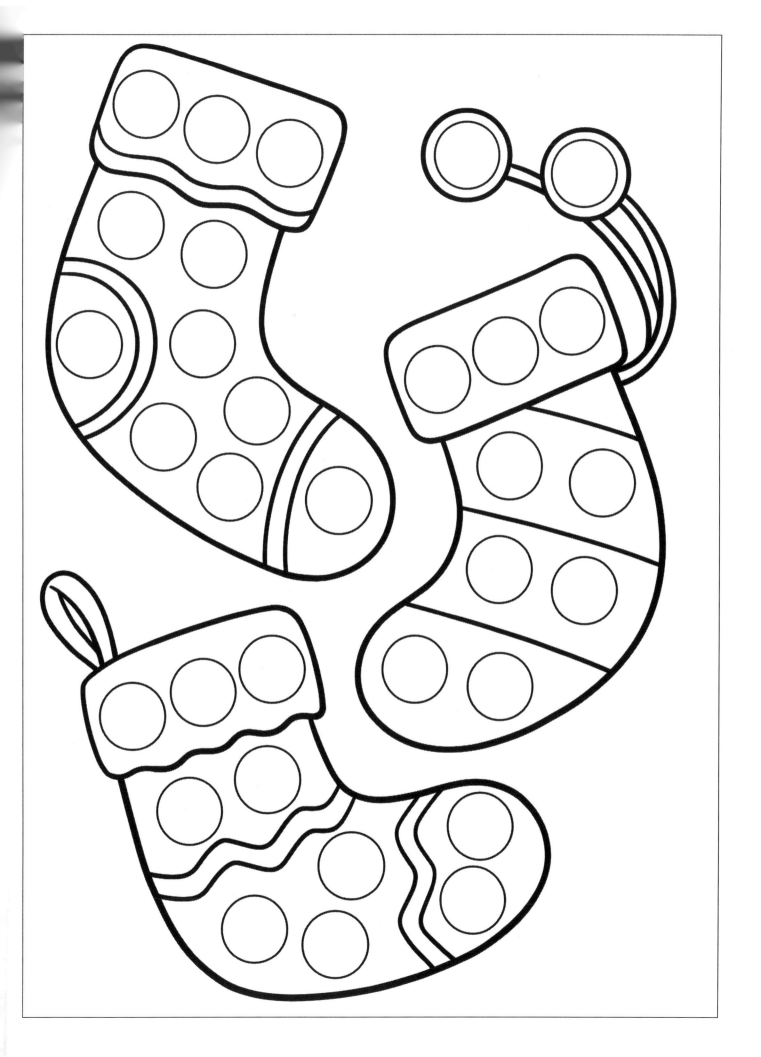

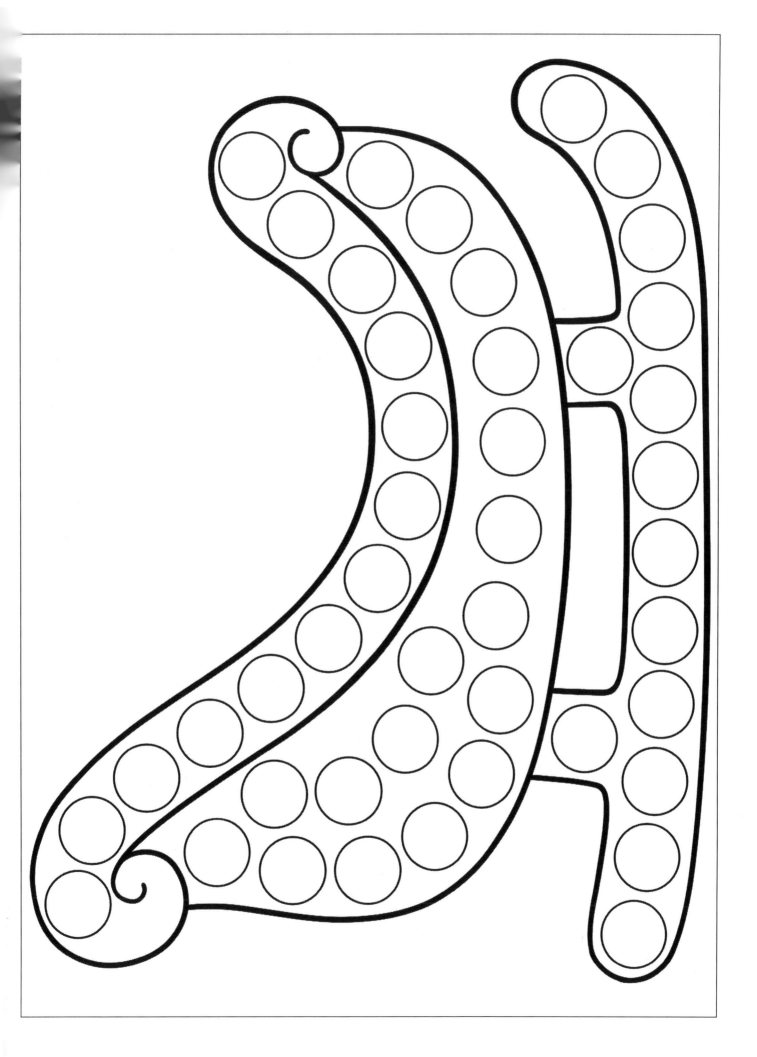

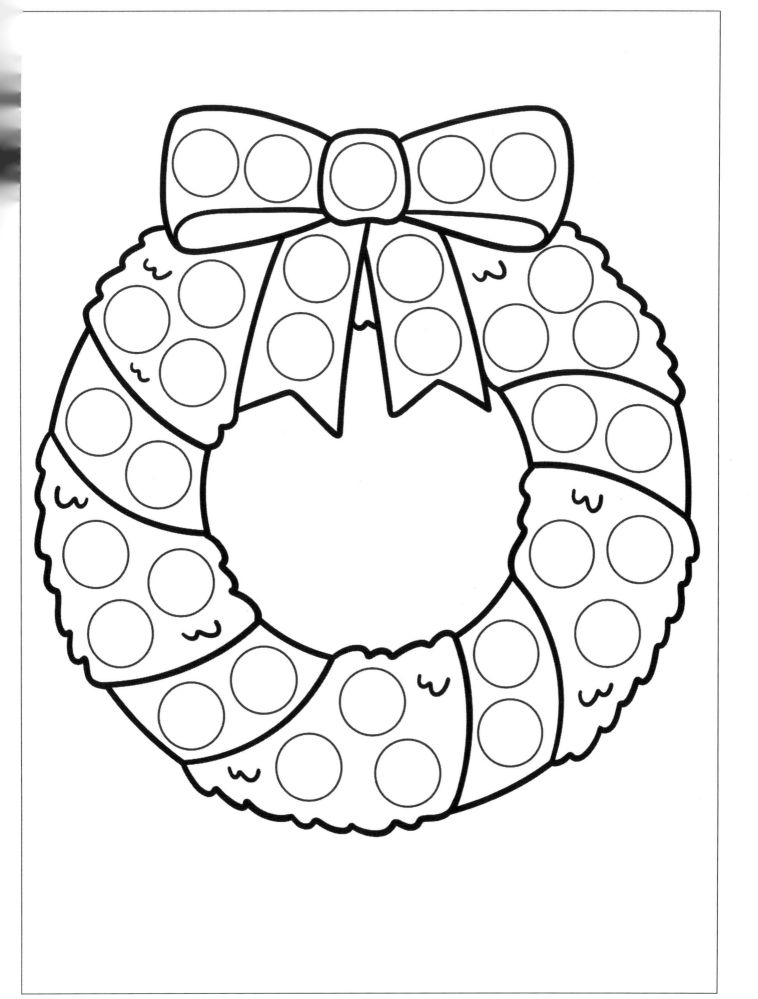

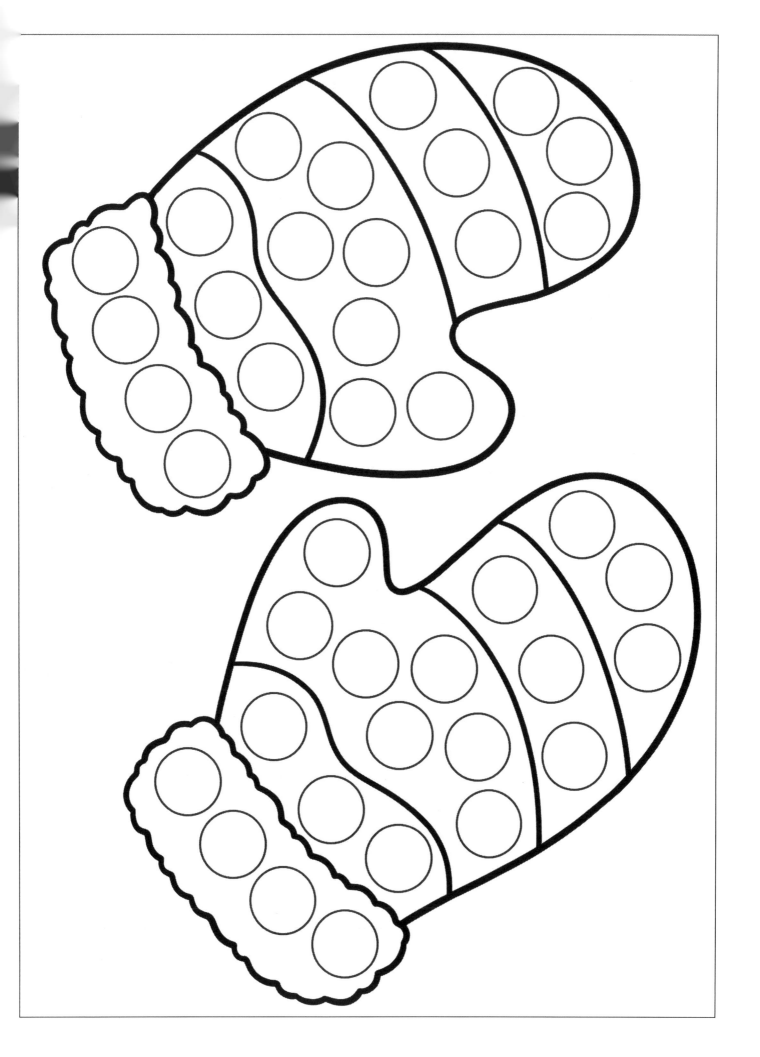

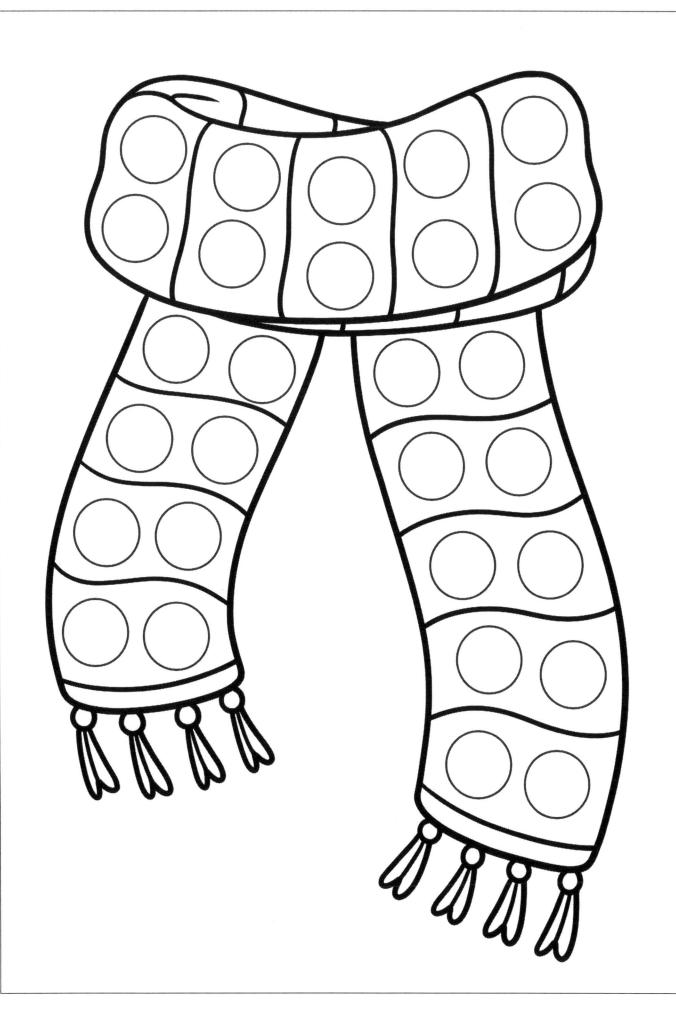

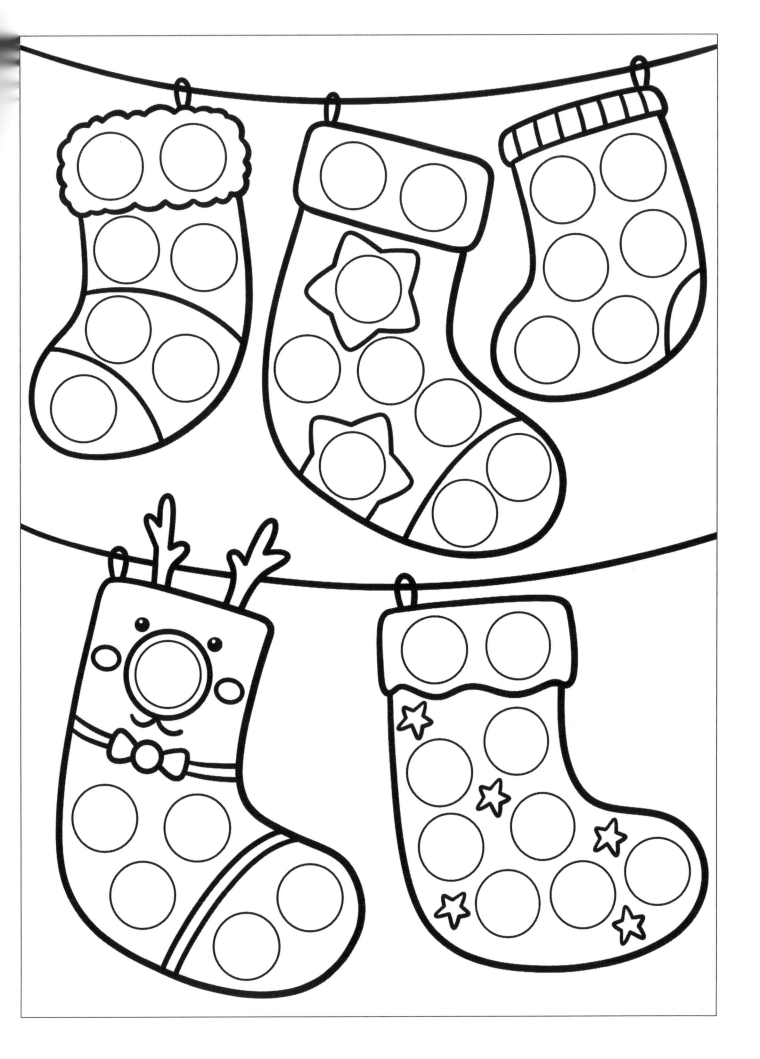

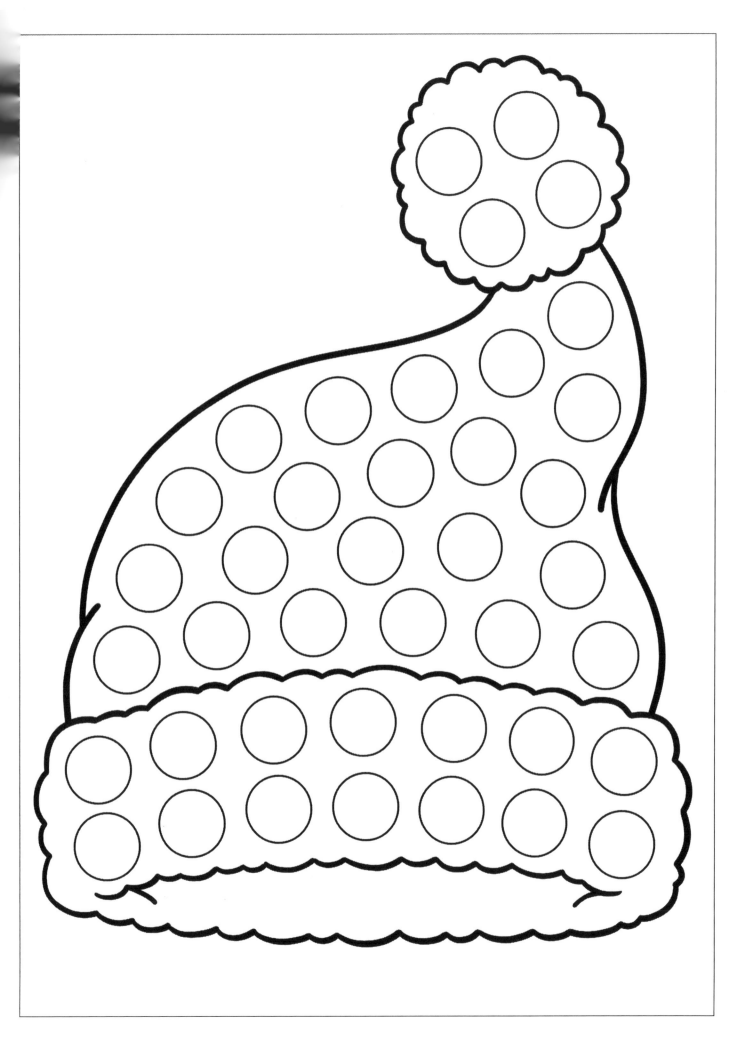

Made in the USA
Las Vegas, NV
23 November 2024

12502553R00048